EVERGREEN

Tabletops

EVERGREEN
Tabletops

ROBERT WAITE

WITH LYNN ARAVE

PHOTOGRAPHS BY ZAC WILLIAMS

GIBBS SMITH
TO ENRICH AND INSPIRE HUMANKIND

First Edition
16 15 14 13 12   5 4 3 2 1

Text © 2012 Robert Waite
Photographs © 2012 Zac Williams

Published by
Gibbs Smith
P.O. Box 667
Layton, Utah 84041

1.800.835.4993 orders
www.gibbs-smith.com

Designed by Sheryl Dickert
Printed and bound in Hong Kong
Gibbs Smith books are printed on paper produced
from sustainable PEFC-certified forest/controlled
wood source. Learn more at www.pefc.org.

Library of Congress Cataloging-in-Publication
Data available upon request

ISBN 13: 978-1-4236-3078-4

To LeAnn Arave and Anita Heaston for their
invaluable help and creative talents.
To my beloved feline family: Jackie, Sister, Jimmy,
and Johnny, who bring such light into my life.
And to my sister, Marilee, who is
so beautiful and talented.

CONTENTS

❖

Introduction 9

Traditional Evergreens 21

Formal Occasions 43

Natural Settings 61

From Unique to Whimsical 81

Inspiration from Tabletop Evergreens 105

Acknowledgments 125

Source Guide 126

Introduction

erhaps no other natural decorations are as versatile and long-lasting as evergreens. True to their name, they may be enjoyed 365 days a year. This book, a companion to *Decorating with Evergreens,* will hopefully inspire you to decorate with evergreens throughout the year and especially outside the traditional "holiday" season time frame. In one sense, the fragrance and greenery of evergreens can help you have a taste of the holidays year-round. There are few restrictions on where you can place an evergreen and the variety of adorning decorations is as wide as your imagination. An evergreen is the "anywhere" style of decoration.

FACING: The Floral Shop for Designer Associates, a full-service flower business. Though small in size, it specializes in "one-of-a-kind," unique floral arrangements, and designed all the floral creations used in this book.

RIGHT: Pink roses, red carnations, white spider mums, green 'Kermit' mums, juniper, princess pine and balsam fir combine for a colorful arrangement.

Designer Associates excels at combining fresh flowers, fruit and live greenery to create fabulous wreaths, garlands, centerpieces, swags, etc., in any season and any setting. Utilizing live plants in arrangements is a very satisfying endeavor and mixing various flowers together will make them even livelier.

One of our main rules is to "do whatever feels good" in creating evergreen decorations. Another of our rules is—"Don't overthink!" "When we do stuff, we don't think about it too much, or it ruins it," Waite stresses. We don't derive instructions from books or on-line or even follow strict orders from customers on how to arrange flowers. We simply follow our hearts and instincts and create in a unique style.

This floral work table showcases a variety of unique and beautiful arrangements. The range of containers adds to the unusual styles, making for "one-of-a-kind" specialty centerpieces.

One recent customer said, "I tell him what we need and they know exactly what I want, and it always turns out perfect!"

We define such an approach as "hometown folk art."

What some may classify as worthless weeds—like thistles and pods—we carefully gather and use enhance our evergreens, finding new uses for what some consider trash.

We favor utilizing the imagination by using things at hand and ingredients in-season and available in your own locale to create decorations to warm the heart and demand attention from your eyes.

Our style is also keenly organic, using such simple things as sheaths of wheat from a farmer's field or crabapples discarded from a neighbor's tree.

ABOVE: This countertop is loaded with different completed arrangements. Some of them are "made to order," using the customer's own vases or memorabilia, which enhances the individual personality of the piece.

FACING: This batch of festive holiday centerpieces is waiting to enliven the homes and businesses of local customers.

Floral heaven

Just walking into this floral shop eases
even the gloomiest of days, with its
brightness, colors and scents.

FACING: The true functionality of a floral shop is usually evident by its wide array of available plants and flowers, as well as by its assortment of fragrances and aromas.

RIGHT: This small bouquet, bursting with vibrant colors, is showcased by being elevated closer to eye level by several brightly colored boxes.

High monetary expense is also not Waite's style. He prefers to prowl local thrift stores for possible vases, pots or baskets. What others see as worthless containers to discard, he envisions as holders of the bounty of nature's beauty and variety in greenery and flowers.

Waite says that purchasing vases from thrift stores will save on at least half of the purchase price as buying brand new. For baskets, the savings will likely be even greater.

Early American settlers had to make do with what they had, and tight economies today foster that same attitude.

Waite's arrangements show how different weights, colors, shapes and textures can combine to create a feeling ranging from the casual to the cheery to the formal.

He urges others to experiment, to try to create what their imagination may dictate. You may be surprised how well nature organizes itself in your hands to produce a unique creation worthy of a lengthy displays.

These flower arrangements are now ready to adorn homes, for an assortment of holidays and occasions—birthdays, anniversaries, welcome homes, bon voyages and so forth.

TRADITIONAL EVERGREENS

*E*vergreens are one of the simplest of creations that can magnify a focal point of hospitality for a home. To have one on a tabletop is a warm and welcoming sign to greet both friends and family—even in the summer and outside of the holiday season. They make a great focal point for listing your house on the neighborhood "map" of friendliness. For example, if you walk or drive down a street, it is likely the home with an evergreen wreath on its door or porch that seems the most friendly and inviting.

FACING/RIGHT: It's all about the blue! Blue ball ornaments seem to overshadow this kitchen countertop arrangement. The white carnations, white alstroemeria, silver brunia and white sticks all blend nicely with the green cedar and balsam fir.

LEFT: Attractive but not overbearing. This little arrangement includes white larkspur, static eucalyptus, boxwood, juniper and red berries. It adds variety to a room, without dominating.

FACING: Setting a peaceful tone at twilight for a holiday evening, tapered candles add warmth to this seasonal arrangement. Cedar, noble fir, poinsettia, ribbon, 'Kermit' mums, red carnation and brunia add extra magic to this tabletop design.

In more modern times, wreaths have come in religious circles to simply be a symbol of eternal love. An evergreen is a durable plant element that has much longevity, and also seems perfect in Christianity as a symbol that represents immortality.

A wreath's circular design can also be connected as a symbol of eternity, without beginning or end. Fruits or colors added to the wreath can denote the rich variety of God's creations.

Native Americans also had high esteem for the evergreen. They believed the circle shape of an evergreen wreath was sacred and called it, "the sacred hoop." Such circular designs represented a fellowship and that all were on the same level and could join hands and work for the common good.

Glass menagerie

A variety of clear and colored glassware, accented by red carnations and a red rose gives this arrangement a unique look. Noble fir, princess pine, pittosporum, 'Safari Sunset', white spider mum, white alstroemeria, *Leptospermum* and silver balls sit on a mirrored tray.

FACING: Composed of pink larkspur, stock and roses, white cushion poms, noble fir, variegated pittosporum and aluminum wire twists in a large silver vase, this elegant arrangement enhances any room.

BELOW: Daylilies, white button poms, 'Safari Sunset' and genista (or sweet broom) mixed with princess pine, cedar and pinecones make up this large, beautiful centerpiece. A perfect arrangement for a formal occasion, it contrasts superbly with a white tablecloth.

This bounty of pineapple, oranges, grapes, limes, lemons and strawberries is mixed with cedar and pine to create a modern "king's table" on this kitchen counter. So appealing it is that perhaps anyone coming into the kitchen will be tempted to eat fruit instead of a less healthy snack or treat. Rotate or rearrange the fruit to keep it fresh and inviting.

Even if you are not the religious type, wreaths convey a simple, hometown charm. They are a timeless symbol of love and friendship. Indeed, technologies will expand by leaps and bounds over the ages ahead, but evergreens will likely still be there and perhaps even expand their warm, inviting legacy.

Circular delight

A topiary wreath made of cedar, princess pine, balsam fir, pepper berries and pinecones and graced with burgundy satin ribbon is a pleasing addition to any table or countertop.

Noble fir and cedar is the base for this pretty centerpiece that's impressive on any dining room table. White cushion poms, solid yellow aster, red roses, carnations, alstroemeria and white roses complete the design.

Tabletop evergreens can go most anywhere. Besides some of the more common places they can be seen, like a fireplace mantel, adorning a beautiful piano, a formal dining room table, or a coffee table, they may also sit in a windowsill, on a desktop, on a kitchen counter and even in a corner by a bathtub.

They can also bring life to any dresser, a wooden chest and even part of a wooden patio swing. One could say a tabletop evergreen is any arrangement up off the floor. Evergreens go with almost anything.

While the "king's table" idea of decorating could be defined by any kind of evergreen combined with all types of fruit available in a particular area, today the world is your garden. You can create a majestic tabletop centerpiece with such fruits as pineapples, grapes, oranges, strawberries, and so forth—an ample assortment that could only be dreamed of in ages past.

Mood lifter

The cedar and sprengeri allow it to drape down the front. Besides the red roses, there are pink daylilies, genista and pinecones for an extra dose of color and shape. Aluminum wire twists add additional flare to a cornucopia of nature's cream of the crop.

Sizzling red roses make this arrangement worthy of any ceremony in a church or home.

ABOVE: There's a holiday surprise of color in this pretty ceramic box. Noble fir, red pixie carnations, green 'Kermit' mums and ruscus combine to set a festive and heart-warming mood.

RIGHT: Did Santa's sleigh lose its load here? Scotch broom, cedar, noble fir, green 'Kermit' mums and spider mums, plus red carnations and white statice surround a cute little Santa bear for the holiday season. This arrangement would work great in a room that lacks a Christmas tree or extensive holiday decorations.

A traditional centerpiece highlights this dining room table. Comprised of pink roses, red carnations, white spider mums, green 'Kermit' mums, princess pine, balsam fir, juniper gold balls and black ting tings, this arrangement will please for breakfast, lunch or dinner.

Ageless beauty

RIGHT: Like an ageless beauty, this arrangement complements this vintage setting with its princess pine, variegated pittosporum, white *Limonium,* red hypericum berries, white alstroemeria, red carnations and white larkspur.

FACING: This overflowing basket dresses up a kitchen table, full of orange lilies, roses, alstroemeria, seeded eucalyptus, juniper, noble fir, Italian ruscus and pinecones.

FORMAL OCCASIONS

*E*ven though it may not be Christmas or the holiday season, a fancy table-top evergreen can be a part of any special event. Evergreens will seem familiar, and their fragrance and presence will warm the hearts of all, invoking joy and peace. The center of a dining room table might be the most popular spot for an evergreen arrangement for your formal occasion.

You're probably not serving just mac-and-cheese with this fine S-shaped arrangement on your dinner table. Cedar pine, oregonia white spider mums, button poms, red hypericum berries and pinecones comprise this floral blockbuster.

Best-dress dinner?

Guests are going to want to be wearing their finest to match this formal centerpiece that adds to the elegance of the fanciest of table settings. Whatever the cuisine, it will likely taste better as diners enjoy this beautiful floral masterpiece.

Some men may believe they are unaffected by a tabletop evergreen—too macho for their fragrance or charm—to calm their soul. But that's usually not so. The aroma of an evergreen demands attention, and one adorned by colorful fruit or flowers will likely soften the hardest of hearts.

If you don't think you can create a fancy enough tabletop evergreen decoration for a special event, consider "cheating" by accenting the container the arrangement is in. For example, put the evergreen atop a silver serving tray. That will add a formal atmosphere to any configuration. Other containers to consider include a shiny brass pot, a fancy jar or a special water pitcher.

LEFT: What's this? White branches soar heavenward in this simple wintery arrangement atop a wooden stand. Balsam fir is the base, while white shade makes a dusting over the fir and pinecones.

FACING: A bright gold vase holds a large dose of eucalyptus, cedar, noble fir, 'Safari Sunset', pepper berries, hypericum berries, variegated carnations and fancy ribbon, which add a kingly atmosphere to any tabletop.

A Midas touch for formal occasions

Majesty times two!

ABOVE: Similar centerpiece and mantelpiece creations enhance, but don't overwhelm, the look of this formal dining room. However, together they foster an elegant atmosphere that's worthy of a royal dinner.

FACING: Countering winter doldrums, the bright red roses and carnations convey anything but the frigid season on this likely holiday-time tabletop. The red flowers accent the red in the snowman's stocking hat design on the plate, while the green 'Kermit' mums tie in with the green napkins. The princess pine, genista and pinecones signal this household will be eating well tonight. The silver aluminum twists highlight the silver charger plates.

FACING: Nature's chorus? This elegant baby grand piano is highlighted by this magnificent display of yellow oncidium orchids, pincushion protea and 'Safari Sunset' mixed with pinecones and noble fir. Any piano player will sound better with this nearby, as the colors explode with beauty.

RIGHT: Elegance for any formal occasion. This large silver bowl is adorned with silver balls and tings, cedar, balsam fir, princess pine and juniper. Green spider mums, 'Kermit' mums, white daylilies and burgundy carnations will make any dining table shine with stature and prestige.

Pink rose charmer

LEFT: A simply beautiful arrangement with larkspur buds, curly willow, and cedar pine, anchored by stunning pink roses in a fancy square vase.

FACING: This deep purple and gold arrangement has a formal elegance that demands to be the centerpiece of any gathering. Purple lisianthus, white roses, pink carnations and purple alstroemeria, plus cedar, balsam fir, Scotch broom, natural tings and golden pinecones all add to its royal nature.

Add roses for a splash of red for the birthday or anniversary of a spouse or family member. Placing a small arrangement on top of a few stacked boxes covered in colorful gift wrapping paper adds both height and exaggeration to your evergreen.

Fit for a king

LEFT: "Ho-Ho-Ho" to this holiday basket full of variegated carnations, snow berries, red and blue satin balls and pinecones. Throw in some Santa figurines, cedar and fir for some extra holiday spirit.

FACING: A star of the holidays, this arrangement has red alstroemeria, balsam fir, *Leptospermum* and glittered stars. It's a perfect display for any windowsill.

If the occasion is less formal, you might consider using an old sugar or flour jar, or an old bucket. Adding a stuffed animal to the mix of flowers and evergreens might make it appeal more to children.

Holiday decorations mixed in will add significance to anything created around Christmas. Adding a few candles will make an evergreen more advent oriented and will give you the option of carefully lighting the candles. You don't even need to add holiday decorations directly to an evergreen. Just sit them around your flowery creation on the same table or stand. A small sleigh is also a great container for an evergreen during the Christmas season.

Since so many households use artificial Christmas trees, putting a small tabletop evergreen in the same room as your holiday tree will add the fragrance of the real thing, but without the mess, cost or effort of having a real tree.

ABOVE: Like Cinderella, a plain tin bucket is transformed into unforgettable beauty with red carnations, cedar, eucalyptus, fir, apples and pinecones.

LEFT: A trio of reindeer usher in the holidays with beautiful cedar, fir, seeded eucalyptus, berries, pinecones, apples and tiny presents.

Lime green is the theme for this centerpiece

ABOVE: Green spider mums, yellow daisies and balls, balsam fir and boxwood combine to make a pleasant atmosphere for any formal occasion.

FACING: What a matchless way to adorn this antique upright piano than with this lovely arrangement of evergreens and protea. The way the branches dangle over and cover the entire top of the piano, it is as if it wants to create its own brand of beautiful music.

NATURAL SETTINGS

*A*ll-natural materials make eco-friendly sense these days. Sometimes, you just can't improve on Mother Nature! Anyone with a single pine tree (or more) in their yard can easily collect pinecones in a bucket as they fall throughout the year and then have them readily available for use in an evergreen or other floral creation. In fact, one wife trained her husband to save fallen pinecones from the yard in a special bucket instead of simply discarding them.

FACING: Nesting in paradise, this cardinal knows how to pick a beautiful home. Red billy balls, pinecones, red and blue ribbon, princess pine and balsam fir add to the charm of this bird-lover's delight.

LEFT: A window to nature: Juniper, lotus pods, Scotch broom, black-eyed Susan pods, red berries and red cardinals in a wire basket combine to brighten up a room with colorful, natural elements from the outdoors. The arrangement shines against the white window no matter the weather.

There are also many plants and flowers that can be collected in the summer and fall, and then hung up to dry. Yarrow, statice, rose hips, pyracantha, sunflower pods, black-eyed Susan pods, are many of the options. You only need to look right outside your door—well, almost.

A variety of ribbon and some floral foam, as well as a hot glue gun, are handy supplies to have on hand for whenever you set out to create your own unique evergreen arrangement. (Do not use Styrofoam to hold flowers, because it does not hold water, as floral foam does, and the flowers will dry out prematurely.)

A quick trip to your local grocery store or market will provide colorful nuts or fruits to give your creation color and interest. Some fruits can be sliced and dried; others actually give some character dried and shriveled.

The variety of greens you can use is numerous. Fir, balsam, juniper, pine, cedar, as well as other types like boxwood, magnolia, holly, eucalyptus and salal can make great accents. A combination of these materials in traditional, as well as nontraditional, ways is encouraged.

Simply simple, and simply wonderful!

LEFT: This modest arrangement of 'Safari Sunset', balsam fir and apples in a terra-cotta pot brings a splash of pizzazz to any pantry. Even if the apples vanish, the joy of nature will remain.

FACING: A fireside basket overflows with balsam fir, apples, oranges, Indian corn, lotus pods and 'Safari Sunset' to liven up any kitchen.

ABOVE: Poinsettia plants for the holiday season top this wicker sleigh just in time for Christmas. Old Saint Nick couldn't have picked a better combination with long-needle pine, juniper, fir, pinecones and ribbon.

FACING: Picture perfect! No one will want to have their picture taken in front of this mantel, in awe of being overshadowed by this fabulous tabletop evergreen. Red roses, white calla lilies and white 'Safari Sunset' warm up an already beautiful brick hearth. With cedar, princess pine, magnolia leaves and variegated pittosporum mixed in as well, who needs a fire going too?

FACING: Noble and balsam fir and ivy allow these apples and lemons to glow freely along the counter, creating a bounty of nature that dominates any tabletop and hopefully a table enough large to contain it.

LEFT: Yellow spider mums, red daisies and solid yellow aster complete this spacious work of art. The metal milk can adds a rustic look.

What a spread!

Fruit-wise, it depends on what's in season in your area. Choosing fruits and vegetables that are in season will keep the cost to a minimum. Apples, for example, can be added to an evergreen in the fall and early winter. Small oranges will work too. Eventually they will need to be replaced, but that's an easy chore. And, if you have a hungry household, they may take away the fruit and consume it, since it will look more attractive in its evergreen setting. In fact, I created an evergreen arrangement for a local restaurant some time ago. It included perishable fruit. I was very surprised many months later to find my creation was still there, looking fresher than ever. Employees had simply been replacing the fruit as needed, giving it a very long shelf life.

During the Middle Ages, in portions of Europe, evergreens were commonly adorned with apples in December and called a "paradise tree." They were representative of Adam and Eve on Christmas Eve each year. The ancient Roman harvest festivals promoted evergreen branches as gifts and symbols of health and strength.

FACING: Spectacular window box. Pyracantha berries are the highlight of this arrangement. Blue juniper, princess pine, balsam fir and pinecones all add to its natural setting and beauty.

ABOVE: Bird's nest on the river? An undersea garden flavor highlights this corner of the room. River pebbles fill this glass vase to create a natural bed of balsam fir for this cute bird. Twigs, pinecones, small red berries complement the nest, while a little white shred provides a fallen snow look to this arrangement.

LEFT: An aging water pitcher is made anew by gerbera daisies, *Leucadendron,* solid yellow aster, pittosporum, cedar and black-eyed Susan pods. This centerpiece will refresh the corner of any kitchen.

FACING: What a charmer! This arrangement can brighten any heart or mood with a beautiful spray of color. Providing the natural fireworks to this basket are yellow daylilies, lemons, white carnations, pink pixies, poms, alstroemeria, ruscus, Scotch broom, seeded eucalyptus, fir, pinecones and curly willow.

Out with the old and in with the new

When it is time to discard or retire your tabletop evergreen,

it is also probably worth the time to see what, if anything,

can be salvaged for possible use in a future floral creation.

ABOVE: This triple-play centerpiece can be used as a grouping or individually, depending on the size of your table. The topiary (ball), made of mini pinecones, is a great conversation piece and stands above the rest.

FACING: Red pixie carnations, apples and candles, with noble fir poking through, comprise this centerpiece that works well for just about any setting or occasion.

ABOVE: A box full of holiday delights graces this table. A simple red bamboo container with holly and pinecones proclaims Merry Christmas to even the toughest of Ebenezer Scrooges.

FACING: The simplest of wooden crates can be brought to life with a touch of princess pine, cedar, juniper, noble fir, pinecones, pepper berries and cardinal birds.

Peaceful splendor

ABOVE: Budding tree branches seem to reach out to the room with their peaceful atmosphere in this tabletop creation. Orange pixie carnations, berries, pinecones, juniper and balsam pine fill this unique rope and berry basket.

FACING: This arrangement graces the edge of this tabletop. Its cedar, holly, brunia Silver Spray, noble fir, variegated pittosporum, red pepper berries, princess pine and bergenia combine to soothe any soul.

BELOW: Orange daylilies bring a heartwarming touch to this centerpiece. Add in magnolia leaves, pinecones, bronze balls, aluminum wire twists, cedar and fir and it creates a fabulous bloom to any tabletop, in any season and for just about any occasion.

FACING: This cozy little bird's nest adds a touch of nature to this lush evergreen centerpiece. A little cedar, noble pine, orange daylilies, pepper berries and dried sunflower pads add to this slice of the outdoors.

FROM UNIQUE TO WHIMSICAL

*A*re there rules for evergreen creation? There are no rules and this chapter is intended to illustrate that. Not the artsy type? You can still experiment and create something unique that will stand out as an expression of your nature and personality. Evergreens give users a beginning base and go with just about anything. All you've got to do is try. Even if your creation is a bit unorthodox, that will make it stand out all the more and will still likely produce a "wow" from onlookers.

FACING: Christmas magic? This whimsical sleigh is adorned with boxwood, red carnations and berries, white spider mums, button poms and a few small pinecones. The nearby Santa Claus figure adds a touch of fantasy to an already unusual tabletop decoration for the holiday season.

LEFT: This quaint white bowl with green spider mums, red carnations, green 'Kermit' mums, princess pine and seeded eucalyptus brightens up a usually drab corner of the room.

Unusual evergreen creations can be great centerpieces in your living room and will be the icebreaker to conversation.

Your evergreen can be as large or small as you like. It can be small enough to put in the thinnest of flower vases, or it can spread out in an oversized wicker basket. An atypical container for an evergreen may be all you need to create your own unique tabletop of flowers. I often search for containers others would throw out—old metal milk jugs, rustic buckets, wooden crates and the like.

Other unusual elements could be different-shaped twigs, and small tree or plant branches. Again, some may trim and throw these away, but they can add a unique character to evergreens.

The only real limit is your imagination. Say you have a plain-looking water vase or water pitcher available to house your flowers and evergreen. If you slice up a few oranges, for example, and fill the bottom of the pitcher with them suspended in the water, you have added color and mystique to the ordinary.

LEFT: This elegant swan will dance its way across any fancy tabletop. An unusual mixture of holly, boxwood, white spider poms and red berries is a plus for any area of the home.

FACING: Blue delphinium and ribbon highlight this silver basket with a splash of red alstroemeria and white spider mums. Cedar and Italian ruscus finish this lovely arrangement.

FACING: Red in red. A bright red vase pops with vivid color thanks to red carnations, berries and floral ting. Mixed in with princess pine, cedar, balsam, silver bells and a few pinecones, here's a unique arrangement to sit on an antique chair or in just about any setting.

LEFT: With a simple but lovely oriental look, this arrangement boasts black floral ting, lotus pods, red roses, juniper and small eucalyptus. It also conveys the illusion of reaching for the sky with swirls of energy.

An exclamation point of nature

LEFT: Polka-dot ribbons add a playful nature to this tabletop concoction. White and red carnations, silver floral ting, balsam fir and miniature presents create a "look at me!" aspect for any room.

FACING: This topiary climbs straight from a white container in a tall, two-layer fashion. Red pixie carnations, variegated pixie carnations, white *Limonium,* balsam fir and boxwood create an eye-catching proportion.

How long does it take to create a tabletop evergreen, such as some of the ones in this book? It depends on many factors, but once you have all the ingredients and supplies, it can require as little as ten to fifteen minutes, or as much as one hour or so.

LEFT: The colorful star of the kitchen. Red carnations, cedar pine and white statice are topped with three red stars to polish off this creation.

FACING: Noble fir, white carnations, purple statice *Limonium* and wire twists are all enhanced by a base of bright, assorted ball ornaments, perfect on any tabletop for the holiday season.

Another consideration, especially if you may end up believing that your evergreen arrangement isn't good enough, is to consider adding some "accessories" to the table and near the evergreen. For example, a seasonal figurine, a stuffed animal or decorative lights placed nearby can enhance it. You may also want to put your arrangement on a fancy or mirrored tray, especially if the occasion is more formal.

Still another possibility is to get a friend or relative to help you create your first evergreen arrangement. Two heads are better than one.

A fancy Christmas delight

ABOVE: A quaint yellow pot serves as an eye-catching vessel atop a fancy table.
Fresh lemons combined with orange daylilies, solid yellow aster, scabiosa pods,
princess pine and pinecones create an unforgettable arrangement.

FACING: A taste of Florida country charm. Blue delphinium, orange roses, pixie carnations, thistle
and fir add to a bounty of fresh oranges piled in a previously neglected corner of the room.

This sliced citrus creation takes up very little countertop space. Add fresh cedar and evergreen to it for extra fragrance and you may not think you need to pay for an expensive remodeling job.

ABOVE: Non-alcoholic delight: An oversized brandy snifter is home to cedar, gold berries, pink gerbera daisies and curly willow. This is a great addition to the edge of this table.

FACING: Small, simple delight. This white vase adorns a tiny table, full of orange freesia, ti leaves, foxtail fern and bergenia in a pleasing, unusual arrangement.

A casual rustic look is what this arrangement boasts

Terra-cotta pots filled with pebbles, plus cedar and balsam fir, yellow viking poms and brunia berries grace this outdoor patio.

What a catch!

The fish isn't the prize, so much as natural cedar, juniper, sprengeri, pinecones, lotus pods, black-eyed Susan pods and pepper berries, which complement even an outdoor setting.

It is also always wise to be cautious and keep tabletop evergreens and other floral arrangements out of the reach of both infants and pets.

Can some people be allergic to evergreens? Yes, some medical studies have revealed that as many as one in ten people may have an allergy to evergreens or other mountain trees. That's a fact to keep in mind if someone in the household displays some significant allergy symptoms when an evergreen in present. Also, live plants brought in from the outside may contain molds, something else some people might be allergic to. Keeping an arrangement away from an allergic person's bedroom, or away from an air vent, are two easy things to do that could make a significant improvement for a person's health, but it may come down to this: is an adorable tabletop evergreen worth its beauty and charm, in relation to the allergic reactions it may produce with someone in the household?

A touch of the Tropics

LEFT: Bright red anthuriums add a touch of paradise. Fir and cedar evergreens, seed eucalyptus, 'Safari Sunset', and bear grass in a white vase create a stunning backdrop. Bright red will help the area feel warm, even if the fireplace isn't lit.

FACING: Bells-of-Ireland, brunia berries, cedar and large philodendron ('Spicy dog') leaves create a green floral wonder.

A touch of the Irish in your washroom

Need something non-electric to brighten up a dark shelf?

Variegated pixie carnations, *Leucadendron* and green ball ornaments with Scotch broom and balsam fir will add a spark to an otherwise lackluster shelf.

INSPIRATION FROM TABLETOP EVERGREENS

A bright tabletop evergreen can be an uplifting method to brighten lifestyles—even on dreary, cloudy or stormy days. Their splash of color can serve as a hint of spring and also spark imagination and hope. In the harsh climate of northern Europe, evergreens were at one time believed to possess magical powers—since they remained green despite the cold, icy weather. So, anciently, evergreen was placed on or near a doorway to ward off potential evil.

FACING: Spectacular eye-catcher! This lavish arrangement features white hydrangeas and red roses, larkspur, hypericum berries, with cedar and ti leaves and eucalyptus in a square crystal vase. It proclaims a colorful welcome to all who enter.

LEFT: Who needs Christmas lights? This stunning arrangement of white daisies, red balls and juniper in a tiny holiday mesh basket is simple yet bright. A pair of ceramic swans nearby add extra charm to a pretty tabletop scene.

Elevated, bright beauty

On a pedestal of three colorful boxes, this small centerpiece rises to any occasion with purple daisies, green spider mums, 'Kermit' mums, red alstroemeria, princess pine and cedar.

Evergreens were one of the hardiest plants around and were brought indoors in winter to freshen stale air and to offer a hint of the outside color to return in the spring.

Historically, some Germans, for example, favored having a small evergreen tree sitting just inside their house, or by the front door, as a sign of hope that spring would eventually come despite the bleakness of a nasty winter. We can still benefit much the same way!

How inspiring are tabletop evergreens? A Google search on-line for the words evergreen and inspiration yielded some 109 million results. Of course, not all those references relate to tabletop evergreens, but this high quantity search result still likely means there is a lot of talk around the world about their value.

Evergreens bring joy and comfort. They may inspire people to eat better and always brighten up the room.

Fragrance is also a key effect from evergreens. It smells so wonderful and is an inspiring aroma. Evergreen brings fragrance into your home, as is evidenced by the number of people who have artificial Christmas trees but add a tabletop evergreen.

Nothing evokes more memories of childhood than an evergreen smell— evergreens make it feel like it is Christmas all year.

Evergreens are also beautiful, comforting and make people feel peaceful, calm and happy.

Any fireplace mantel will come alive with natural color

Yellow daylilies, lemons, white carnations, pink pixies, poms, alstroemeria, ruscus, Scotch broom, seeded eucalyptus, fir, pinecones and curly willow all lend their colorful support to this inspiring arrangement.

A basket load of inspiration

ABOVE: A virtual cornucopia of autumn colors, with sunflowers, red daisies, *Leucadendron*, princess pine, balsam fir, apples, oranges, lemons and some fall leaves. This arrangement will brighten up any portion of the home or yard.

LEFT: Yellow daylilies, red carnations, white cushion poms, cedar balsam fir and solid yellow aster are held together by a bright plaid bow in a pleasing tabletop creation.

The longevity of evergreens, especially when they have water, and their wide range of colors add needed color to the winter world in particular, when the colors of white (snow), gray (clouds) and brown (lawns) might dominate the landscape.

How long your creation may last may also center on another simple rule—giving them water. Just misting flowers or plants may enhance their longevity. Misting or watering an evergreen and its accompanying decorations should be done weekly, but it depends on the climate in your area.

Refrain from putting an evergreen near a fan or heater to prevent it from drying out much earlier than it should. Placing an evergreen in direct sunlight should also be avoided, if at all possible.

You will know when an evergreen is too old, because, like a Christmas tree, the needles will begin to fall off as it dries out. Then it is time to discard it, as it will not only be untidy but will be somewhat of a fire hazard.

LEFT: Creating a different kind of tune, red carnations, noble fir, wax flowers and star cookie cutters in a wicker basket can stir the soul with a visual symphony of color and imagination.

FACING: Even if the Mona Lisa was above this striking evergreen arrangement, the evergreen would still hold its own. With its red roses and carnations, plus green 'Kermit' mums, genista, pinecones and princess pines, this is a work of art all its own. The silver aluminum twists and silver ball ornaments further highlight this masterpiece.

LEFT: Guaranteed mood enhancer! This lighted luminary is powered by red roses, eucalyptus, cedar and *Leptospermum* for a gorgeous configuration that will be the talk of the town.

FACING: Seeming to almost defy gravity, this angelic, uplifting arrangement is held aloft by a cherub. Red pixie carnations, red freesia, white alstroemeria, cedar, foxtail and seeded eucalyptus decorate the corner of a room in a heavenly fashion.

Tabletop evergreen arrangements can make great gifts for Christmas, birthdays, anniversaries, and more. Especially if you create one yourself! It is a unique gift and one that may be the perfect alternative for that hard-to-buy-for person who seemingly has everything already. For example, creating an arrangement and including not only a person's favorite flowers but their favorite fruit as well would be sure to please.

While evergreen creations may dominate during the holiday season, another great time for their usage is for Valentine's Day. An evergreen arrangement from the holidays saved for just over a month can be revived and re-used for Valentine's, with some red lights, candles or heart-shaped items.

What's the dominant color for St. Patrick's Day? Green. And, nothing is greener than an evergreen, so it should be considered for use in Irish festivities.

Natural light and a window view

produce a Garden of Eden effect indoors

Mixing flowers and vegetables make this lovely arrangement. Variegated carnations, artichokes, kale, silver brunia, cedar, princess pine, rosemary and red river birch sticks make a truly inspiring natural creation on this end table.

FACING: This small,
but striking nosegay
bouquet, would brighten
up any countertop.
Red carnations, white
cushion poms, cedar
and bear grass, tied with
a pretty red bow make
up this little beauty.

RIGHT: Just what the
doctor ordered! Fresh
flowers can bring color
to any area of the
home. These bright pixie
carnations do just that.
Myrtle cedar and brunia
accent a frosted vase
that puts extra style into
this small but powerfully
inspiring creation.

A welcoming entrance

FACING: What a picture-perfect entryway to this home, thanks to twin evergreen wreaths brightening the doorway.

ABOVE: This classic home is the perfect setting for a myriad of different uses for evergreens.

LEFT & ABOVE: Historic homes such as these often have evergreen trees in their yards, which enable the regular presence of tabletop evergreens. Unique floral wreaths add to the appeal.

FACING: These classic floral wreaths proclaim a strong "welcoming" invitation to all who enter.

Acknowledgments

❦

I would like to thank the following, who allowed the use of their homes or other work/support to help create this book. Without them, this work would not have been possible.

Dennis and Genene Hill	Dan and Kathy Scarborough
Lance and Nancy Reese	Chuck and Emily Montgomery
Norris and Dale Robins	Utah State University Botanical Center,
Scott and Samantha Simpson	Kaysville, Utah
Lorin and Kaye Wild	Lynn and LeAnn Arave
Richard and Carol Major	Anita Heaston
Gaye Rhodes and Janice Ventura	Zac Williams (photographer)

Thanks also go to Mr. Gibbs Smith for his leadership and encouragement on this follow-up project, and to my darling sister, Rula Hunter. Also, grateful appreciation for the readers of the original book in this series, *Decorating with Evergreens*.

Source Guide

———◆———

Y ou can purchase most of your flowers, evergreens and other basic supplies for your tabletop evergreens from your local florist or garden center. You will also find additional items, such as containers, baskets and vases, from a hardware, variety or thrift store. Yard sales are yet another great resource for finding usable and unusual items and containers. A walk into neighboring fields, woods or the countryside may also yield some weeds or flowers that might add spice to your own unique arrangement.

The following suppliers are examples of where catalogs or on-line evergreen and floral supply information may be found:

DENVER WHOLESALE FLORISTS

DWF ALBUQUERQUE
4717 Lumber Avenue NE
Albuquerque, NM 87109
505.888.2636

DWF BOISE
1623 River Street
Boise, ID 83702
208.336.5275
208.344.8938 Fax

DWF CINCINNATI
4725 Ashley Drive
Hamilton, OH 45011
513.874.5183
513.870.5185 Fax

DWF OF COLUMBUS
3707 Interchange Road
Columbus, OH 43204
614.227.7026
888.857.9777

DWF DALLAS
2430 Converse Street
Dallas, TX 75207
214.631.3280
214.634.1593 Fax

DWF DENVER
4800 Dahlia Street
Denver, CO 80216
303.399.0970

DWF FLINT
5100 Exchange Drive
Flint, MI 48507
810.733.5100
810.733.8530 Fax

DWF KANSAS CITY
21 West 13th Avenue
N. Kansas City, MO 64116
816.474.9705
816.842.7342 Fax

DWF MILWAUKEE
425 West Walnut
Milwaukee, WI 53212
414.263.8400
414.263.8407 Fax

DWF OMAHA
10923 Olive Street
Omaha, NE 68128
402.339.5080
402.339.9557 Fax

DWF SALT LAKE CITY
601 West 4330 South
Murray, UT 84123
801.904.4800
800.827.4393
801.904.4807 Fax

DWF SEA/TAC
7327 South 228th Street
Kent, WA 98032
253.854.5800
253.372.3800 Fax

DWF ST. LOUIS
2715 LaSalle Street
St. Louis, MO 63104
314.772.0254
314.772.7800 Fax

DWF TOLEDO
14 North Erie Street
Toledo, OH 43604
419.241.7241
419.241.3828 Fax

ENSIGN WHOLESALE FLORAL

EWF SALT LAKE CITY
461 South 600 East
Salt Lake City, UT 84102
801.359-8746
800.662.3666 Toll Free, In State
800.453.3016 Toll Free, Out of State
801.359.5801 Fax

EWF OGDEN
1167 West 3050 South
Ogden, UT 84403
801.621.7704
888.850.2527
801.621.4798 Fax

ESPRIT WHOLESALE FLORIST

4260 South 500 West
Murray, UT 84123
espritsaltlake.com
888.955.8835
801.281.4695 Fax